"Dammit Janet!"

Sullivan and Trilby wanted me to get this book for you... you see, some of the stories in here were related by their ancestors, and I felt it was only fair since they were the ones who talked to Buster about your birthday (and then told us about it!). Have a fantastic one !?!!@#!!!

YAHOO !!!

Dona + Syd.

Cat Tales

Told By Richard Watherwax

Designed By Philip Lief

A WALLABY BOOK-PUBLISHED BY POCKET BOOKS NEW YORK

To Willoughby

POCKET BOOKS,
a SIMON & SCHUSTER division of
GULF & WESTERN CORPORATION
1230 AVENUE OF THE AMERICAS, NEW YORK, N.Y. 10020

ISBN: 0-671-79075-7

First Wallaby printing   April, 1979

10 9 8 7 6 5 4 3 2

WALLABY and colophon are trademarks of Simon & Schuster

Printed in the U.S.A.

Once upon a time I had an old cat named Willoughby. During his final winter with me he would lie in front of the fire and reminisce about cats he had known. He would laugh and tell some funny stories, and sometimes he would grow silent and think about his old pals. These cat tales are based on what he told me. And all of them are true. His last words to me echo my sentiments—"I never met a cat I didn't like."

-R.W.

THE
CREATIVE
CAT

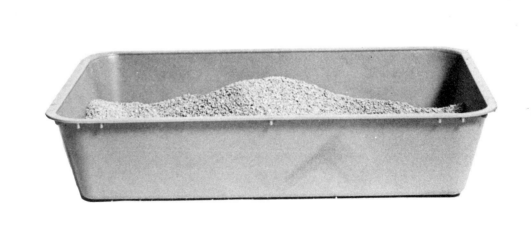

THE HAUNTED HOUSE

Once upon a time, two sisters lived all alone
in a haunted house.

Joan, the older sister, was totally deaf.
But Bette, the younger sister, had fine hearing.

Every night she would hear screeching sounds, moaning and wailing. Now and then the old house would tremble and groan as if in agony.

The sounds were loudest
upstairs in the attic...

where the locked room was.
One night unable to
stand it any longer
she raced up the stairs
into the dark hall.

The locked room was open!
The groaning noises got louder
as she screwed up her courage
and burst through the door...

CATNIP leaves & herbs *with cat play ball*

Training your cat to walk on a leash is simple...
A. attach harness

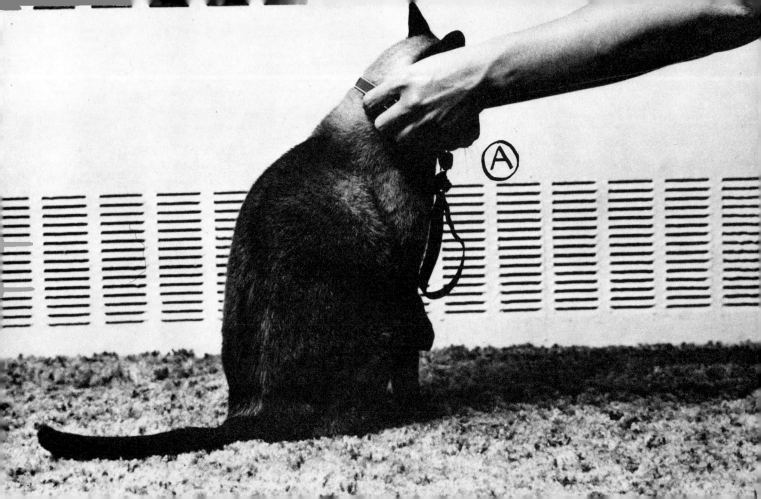

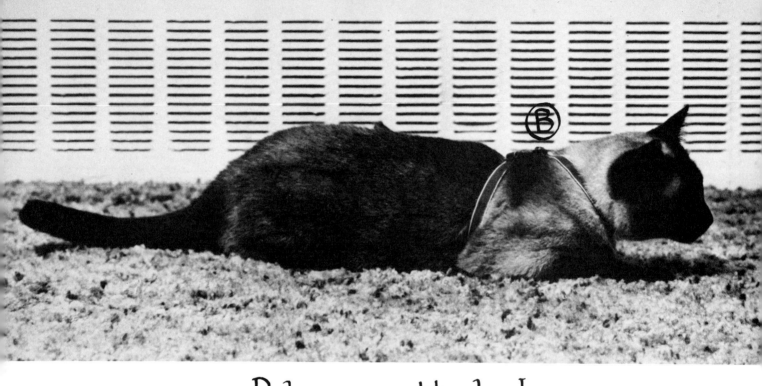

B. harness attached

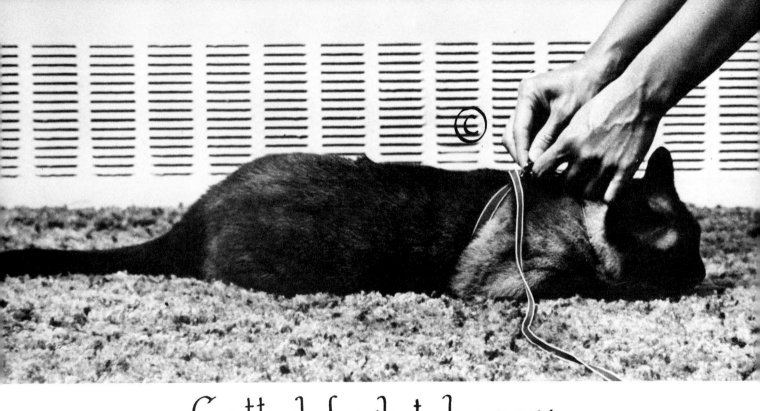

C. attach leash to harness.

D. cat in walking position. Pull firmly on leash

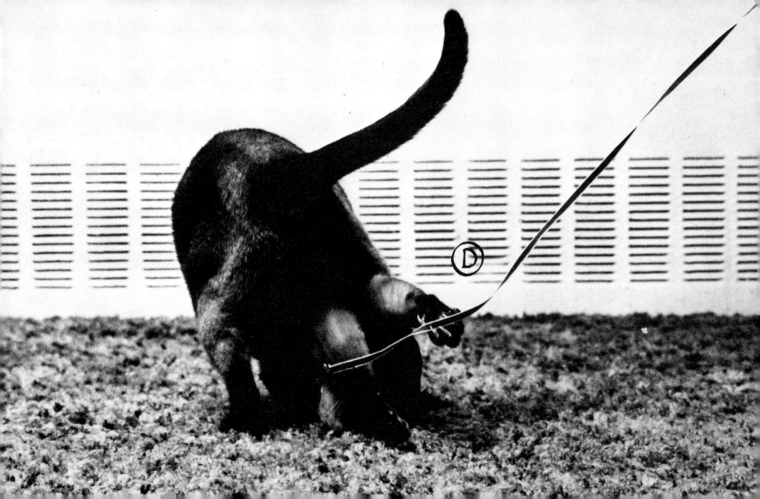

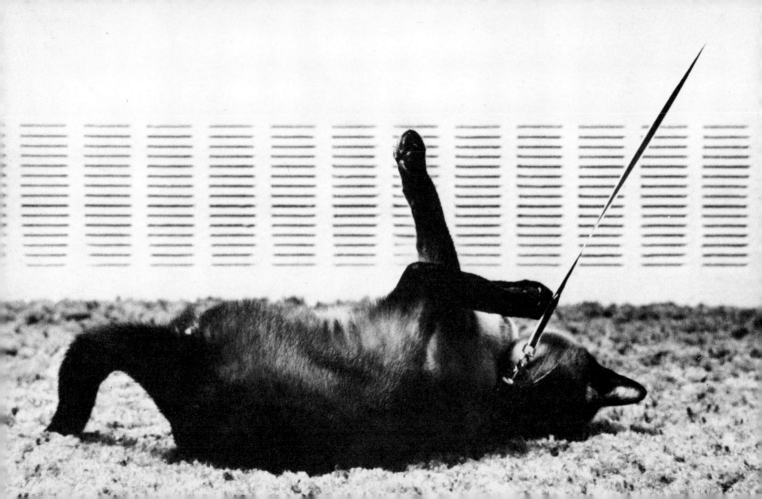

You may have to use a little force.

Cats get bored easily.
Here are five simple ways
you can entertain them...

1. Give your cat flying lessons...

2. Put on a Magic Show...

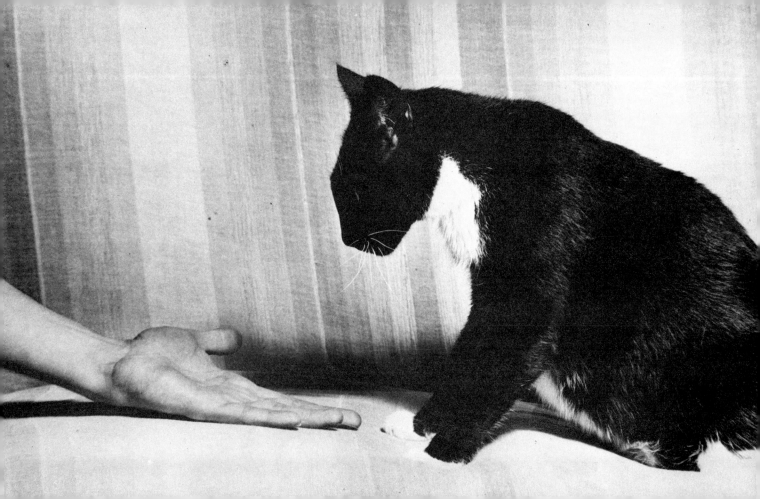

3. Sing To your cat...

 **4.** **Install an artificial Mouse Hole...**

5. Play "Hat the Cat" with them. It's their favorite game...

THE INVISIBLE CAT

CLEAR CONSOMMÉ FOR LUNCH...

MARY'S KITTEN, TOTO, DISAPPEARED INTO THIN AIR...

SHE TRIED TO KEEP TRACK OF IT
BY TYING RIBBONS ON ITS' LEGS AND TAIL.
BUT CATS DON'T LIKE TO WEAR ANYTHING.
BESIDES, IT FRIGHTENED GUESTS.

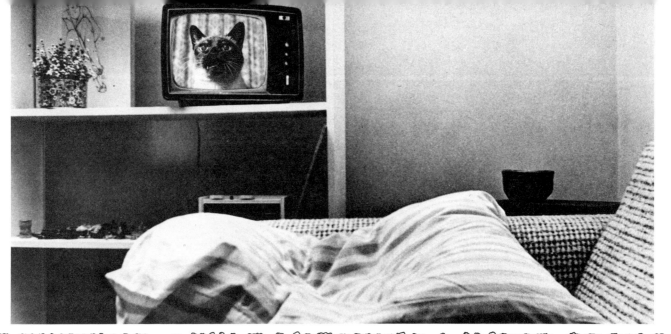

ONE EVENING, WHILE WATCHING WALTER CRONCAT ON THE 6 O'CLOCK NEWS, TOTO HEARD OF A NEW PRODUCT. HE TOLD MARY, AND SHE WENT OUT TO BUY SOME...

SHE FOUND IT AT A NEARBY HARDWARE STORE.
AND IN A FEW QUICK BRUSH STROKES,
SHE HAD HER KITTEN BACK. THEY LIVED HAPPILY
EVER AFTER ... BUT NO MORE CLEAR CONSOMMÉ.

The Peeping Tom Cat

A SHY CAT
HIDING BEHIND
A BUSH

WALTER CRONCAT WRAPS UP THE NEWS...

The 3 Differences Between Cats and People...

1. Cats don't have laps.
2. Cats are never late.
3. Cats don't tell jokes.

However, it has come to our attention,
that in McKeesport, Pa.........

Cats have remarkable eyesight. They can see in the dark, even stare at the sun. One little known reason for their unique vision is...

They wear contact lenses.

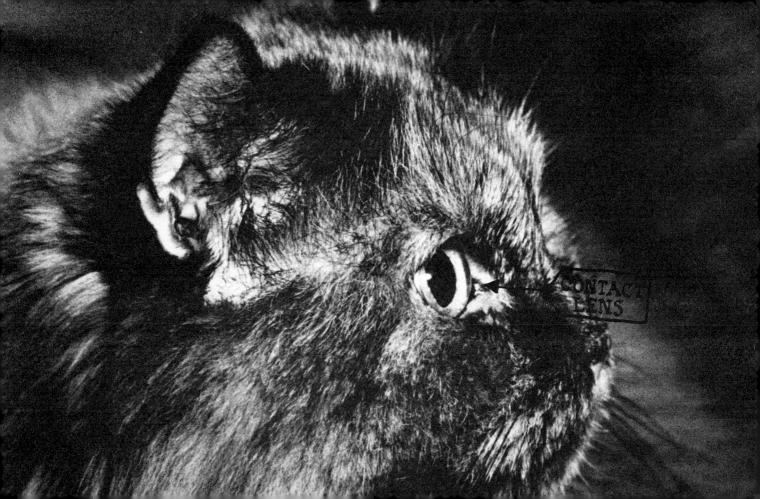

CONTACT LENS

Quite often you'll see your cat washing the lenses before putting them in. Like us, they suffer some of the drawbacks of contacts, such as...

closing a lens.

One Cat's Solution . . .

Cats need an outlet for their energy...

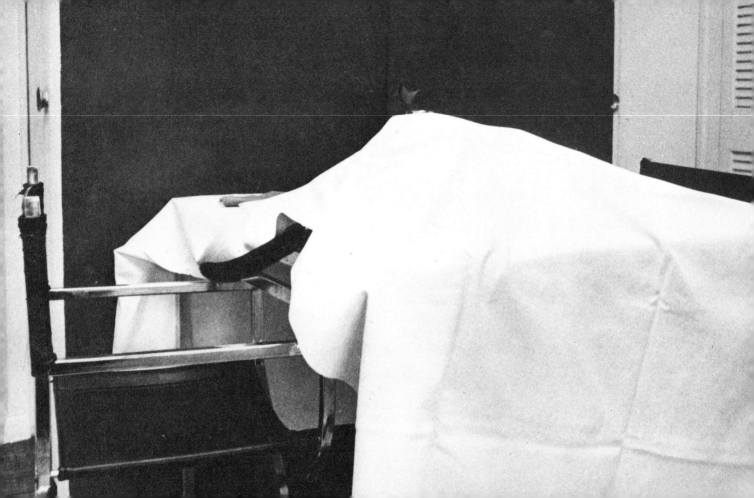

Thousands of dollars are spent annually on "gourmet" cat foods for finicky eaters. If your cat is a picky eater, here is a a suggestion that never fails......

A common disease among fur bearing mammals. The symptoms of ACUTE MANGE are a stiffening of the tail, followed by a loss of fur......

Cats are very resourceful.
When left alone, they can
always amuse themselves...

One Sunday Morning...

A White Cat Iceskating